The CONTRADICTORINESS *of* SIN

Other works by Dr. Surrendra Gangadean & The Logos Foundation:

Philosophical Foundation: A Critical Analysis of Basic Beliefs

History of Philosophy: A Critical Analysis of Unresolved Disputes

Theological Foundation: A Critical Analysis of Christian Belief

Philosophical Foundation: Trivium Study Guide

The Logos Papers: To Make the Logos Known

The Westminster Confession: A Doxological Understanding

The Westminster Shorter and Larger Catechisms: A Doxological Understanding

On Natural and Revealed Theology: Collected Essays of Surrendra Gangadean

The Logos Curriculum: Grammar Catechisms: Philosophical, Theological, and Historical Foundations

Fundación Filosofica: Un Análisis Crítico de Creencias Básicas

DOXOLOGICAL REFORMED SERMON SERIES:

The Book of Revelation: What Must Soon Take Place Doxological Postmillennialism

The Biblical Worldview: Creation, Fall, Redemption Genesis 1–3: Scripture in Organic Seed Form

The Unity of the Church: That They May Be One That the World May Believe

PHILOSOPHICAL FOUNDATION DIALOGUE SERIES:

Introduction to Philosophy: The Basic Things Are Clear to Reason

The
CONTRADICTORINESS
of SIN

A Reading of Paradise Lost

SURRENDRA GANGADEAN

A DIVISION OF THE LOGOS FOUNDATION
Phoenix, Arizona

The Contradictoriness of Sin: A Reading of Paradise Lost

Copyright © 1968, 2024 Surrendra Gangadean

Logos Papers Press 1968, 2024
Phoenix, Arizona
logospaperspress.com

Printed in the United States of America

All rights reserved. No part of this publication may be reproduced, stored in a retrieval system, or transmitted in any form or by any means—electronic, mechanical, photocopy, recording, scanning, or otherwise—without the prior written permission from the publisher, Logos Papers Press. It is illegal to copy this book, post it to a website, or distribute it by any other means without permission.

Scriptures quotes are taken from the KING JAMES VERSION (KJV): KING JAMES VERSION, public domain, except where cited.

Cover Design: Beth Ellen Nagle
Typesetting: Matthew P. Hicks & Brian J. Phelps

Library of Congress Cataloging-in-Publication Data pending

Gangadean, Surrendra, 1943–2022.
    The contradictoriness of sin: a reading of paradise lost
    Includes bibliographical references
    ISBN: 979-8-9898295-0-7 (hbk.)
    ISBN: 979-8-9898295-1-4 (e-book)

1. John Milton 2. Sin—Paradise Lost 3. Theology—Critical Analysis of Sin 4. Philosophy of Art 5. Humanities I. Title

For the beauty of holiness

Contents

Introduction ix

The Contradictoriness of Sin: 1
        A Reading of *Paradise Lost*

Appendix A: Existential Hermeneutics: 37
        Prolegomena to Philosophy of Art

Appendix B: Philosophy of Art Outline 53

Selected Bibliography 55

About the Author 59

INTRODUCTION

DR. SURRENDRA GANGADEAN, AT AGE 24, wrote his thesis for the Master's Degree in English Literature on January 16, 1968. Dr. Gangadean had mentioned its existence in private conversations and sermons, but with his customary modesty and humility, the work remained undisclosed during his lifetime. Since it is now in the possession of the Logos Archives, we have had the opportunity to analyze its content and unanimously agree on its merit. The publication of this work will aid in tracing the intellectual journey of Dr. Gangadean's foundational ideas, which shaped his later contributions. Additionally, it will be invaluable for future scholars' research into his life and work. This piece provides a prime example of critical literary analysis, employing insights from general revelation to identify what is of lasting value in a literary work. Moreover, it calls attention to the need for a foundation to ground the study of the arts upon prior philosophical and theological methods and presuppositions.

The Contradictoriness of Sin: A Reading of Paradise Lost provides a historical analysis of the development of Dr. Gangadean's ideas. In it, we find the beginnings of his understanding of theodicy (the Ironic Solution),[1] anthropology

---

1. Surrendra Gangadean, *Philosophical Foundation: A Critical Analysis of Basic Beliefs*, Second Edition (Phoenix: Public Philosophy Press, 2022), 156–161; Surrendra Gangadean, *On Natural and Revealed Theology: Collected Essays of Surrendra Gangadean*, (Phoenix: Logos Papers Press, 2023), 141–147.

(triune personality),² theology (the doxological focus),³ and literary analysis (liberal humanism). These elements remained constant in his thinking and were developed further in subsequent works. The consistency and continuity of his thinking from such an early point in his academic career are remarkable. At that time, Dr. Gangadean was just beginning his philosophical, theological, and literary studies; he was unacquainted with the Historic Christian Faith and had yet to formulate Rational Presuppositionalism and other supportive doctrines.

Consistent with Dr. Gangadean's focus on foundation, he embarked upon a daunting task by seeking to understand the nature of sin concretely depicted in one of the most challenging characters in literature and the Bible. In Milton's Satan, he found an accurate portrayal of sin that is not limited to unrighteousness as commonly conceived,⁴ but reaches to the core of our being and encompasses the whole person—intellect, emotion, and will. In Satan, sin extends beyond unrighteousness to unbelief (believing what is false) and unholiness (devotion to self instead of devotion to God). Sin at its root denies our creatureliness in being finite, temporal, and changeable while denying God's nature as infinite, eternal, and unchangeable. The darkened mind denies the clear difference between the finite (created) and the infinite (Creator). Fundamentally, sin is a denial of our nature as rational, and consequently, it proceeds by denying the clear revelation of the truth of God as structured in the nature of things created. This denial is

---

2. See: *Appendix A: Prolegomena to Philosophy of Art*.

3. Surrendra Gangadean, *The Westminster Confession of Faith: A Doxological Understanding* (Phoenix: Logos Papers Press, 2024).

4. C. S. Lewis, *A Preface to Paradise Lost* (New York: HarperCollins Publishers, 1942), 89–90.

progressive, consistent with our finitude and the unfolding of divine providence.

Milton's Satan is confronted with his ontology (changeable being) and the increased revelation of God's glory in providence. This gives rise to his existential struggle: to remain in autonomy and unbelief requires ever-increasing attempts to deceive and justify himself to avoid seeing what is objectively clear. There lies the basis of the contradictoriness of sin, for Satan is confronted *every step of the way* with the possibility of the alternative—choosing what is good instead of evil. Rather than heeding the many calls to repentance and engaging in reconsideration, reevaluation, and tracing back the folly of his ways, Satan doubles down in his obstinacy and determination to rationalize his rejection of the clear revelation of the truth of God.

Satan becomes a lie personified, an increasingly incoherent being whose claims and arguments collide and sink deeper into contradictoriness. The way forward for Satan is to deny his nature as fundamentally rational and embrace the incoherence of sin, which, in the end, is self-destructive. By clinging to the lie, his intellectual quest concludes with the disintegration of his thinking and the deformation of his being. Sin is total; it is destructive of the whole person; it encompasses thought and being and progressively increases towards deeper and greater degrees of meaninglessness, incoherence, and self-destruction.

Dr. Gangadean possessed an uncanny ability to turn the strongest argument *against* a position into the strongest argument in *defense* of that position. When confronting the problem of evil in David Hume's *Dialogues*, he used Hume's formulation to advance an easy solution, which ironically dissolves the problem of evil.[5] When faced with the rejection of the ontological status of reason in the Enlightenment, Dr. Gangadean launched a reconstruction of reason through Rational Presuppositionalism. This pattern extends to many of his contributions. So here also, he shows the aptitude to use the force of the opposition to formulate an even more compelling response. This may be regarded as *intellectual judo*.

Dr. Gangadean turned what is deemed problematic in Milton's Satan into a case study of how to draw from a literary work the universal elements present in the nature of man. A literary work provides a concrete illustration of human nature that affords the careful analysis and extrapolation of universal elements. The humanizing of Satan should not be considered a failure in Milton's work; in fact, it is a significant achievement because he shows the nature of sin (in both fallen angel and fallen man) as it works itself out in the mind of Satan. By bringing attention to Satan's thinking, Dr. Gangadean set out to show how the humanizing of Satan renders all the more clearly the self-destructive nature of sin at the levels of thought and being. The contradictoriness of sin is inherently self-destructive and, as such, an unlivable condition that can only be endured through increased hypocrisy—self-deception and self-justification, unendingly.

The Contradictoriness of Sin is a concise and insightful analysis of the anatomy of sin. It guides the reader to examine the subtleties of the mind in attempting to distort and obfuscate what is otherwise clear. We come alongside Satan and watch and process his gradual yet restless refusal

---

5. Gangadean, *Philosophical Foundation*, 145–161; Gangadean, *On Natural and Revealed Theology*, 141–147; Surrendra Gangadean, "Paper No. 7: The Problem of Evil," in *The Logos Papers: To Make the Logos Known* (Phoenix: Logos Papers Press, 2022), 33–39.

to submit or yield. This work gives an introspective analysis of sin as a study of human psychology up close; it shows the sinful pattern of our fallen mind in the neglect, avoidance, resistance, and denial of what is clear about God and man, and good and evil.

May this work serve in understanding the conflict between light and darkness in the spiritual war, beginning with oneself.

"In him was life, and that life was the light of men. The light shines in the darkness, but the darkness has not understood it" (John 1:4–5 NIV).

—THE LOGOS FOUNDATION
EDITORIAL BOARD
Phoenix, Arizona
April 2024

The Contradictoriness of Sin

THE CONTRADICTORINESS OF SIN
A Reading of Paradise Lost

SELF-CONTRADICTION CAN OCCUR on two levels: on the level of thought or consciousness and on the level of action or being. At the level of consciousness, self-contradiction entails self-deception; on the level of being, it leads to self-destruction. By self-contradiction, I mean that which is inconsistent with itself and reality in a logical and necessary manner.[1] On the level of either thought or action, self-contradiction may proceed in a willing or unwilling manner. Inevitably, persistence in self-contradiction moves from a willing to an unwilling self-contradiction. On the level of thought, the movement is from using lies which contradict each other to becoming a Lie—a self-contradiction personified. On the level of action, the movement is from that of deceiving to being deceived, from adopting a disguise to becoming that disguise. What is begun willingly in oneself becomes concrete in reality whether one wills or not. As a Lie personified, one is self-deceived; as becoming that which one intended only as a disguise, one is self-destroyed.

In this paper, I would like to show how the Satan of *Paradise Lost* is involved in this type of contradiction, and how it leads to the disintegration of his thinking process

---

1. Self-contradiction develops out of the essential nature of the thought or act in question whereas an error reveals inconsistency by 'accident' (in the Thomistic sense of the word).

and to the deformation of his being. Satan's fall was not due to an error in judgment (else he could have been corrected) but to the contradictoriness of sin which goes beyond the dimension of reasoning to include the dimensions of emotion and will.[2] "What time his pride / Had cast him out from heaven, with all his host / Of rebel angels" (Milton I.36–38) is an instance at the very outset of the epic which embodies the Satanic contradiction. The pride which would have catapulted him into the seat of "heaven's high king" (V.220) has only served to cast him down to the lowest Hell. The result is not a mere failure but total reversal of his expectation. Continuing: "by whose aid aspiring / To set himself in glory above his peers" (I.38–39) forces another set of contradictions upon the reader. In the scale of being established by God, peers will always remain peers and any hope to change things can only satisfy itself in appearances. But to add to the irony of the situation, Satan, not being sufficient in himself to rise above his peers, involves them in self-contradictory action against themselves. And again:

> He trusted to have equalled the most high,
> If he opposed; and with ambitious aim
> Against the throne and monarchy of God
> Raised impious war in heaven and battle proud
> With vain attempt (I.40–44).

The rebellion of a creature against its creator is, as C.S. Lewis puts it, "like the scent of a flower trying to destroy the flower. As a consequence, the same rebellion which means

---

2. "The initial act is an act against nature, it is a primal sin, in that it contradicts the 'essential fact of things', and its author knows that it does so. It is not an act committed by mistake; it is not an error of judgment, it is an error of will." Helen Gardner, *A Reading of Paradise Lost* (Oxford, 1965), 102.

misery for the feelings and corruption for the Will, means Nonsense for the intellect."[3]

In the invocation of Book 1, the poet calls upon the muse to sing "Of MAN'S first disobedience . . ." (I.1), and he calls upon the Holy Spirit to instruct him that he may "justify the ways of God to men" (I.26). In both cases Man is the subject, but in both cases also the activity of Satan is involved: "say first what cause / Moved our grand parents in that happy state . . . Who first seduced them to that foul revolt?" (I.28–29, 33). In treating the first cause of Man's first disobedience, the poet must give an account of Satan's first disobedience—an account which involves peering into the mystery of iniquity. The account must further serve the poet's intention of justifying God's ways to men. The poet depicts Satan, an angelic being of the highest order who, thinking himself "impaired" because Messiah (his creator) has been appointed Head of the Angels, is caught in an attempt to save his life and inevitably ends up losing it. This account, at the other extreme of leaving the Satanic revolt wrapped up in mystery, runs the risk of making Satan into a cosmic buffoon at his own expense. For, to use Mr. Lewis's analysis:

> A being superior to himself in kind, by whom he himself had been created—a being far above him in the natural hierarchy—had been preferred to him in honor by an authority whose right to do so was not disputable, and in a fashion which as Abdiel points out, constituted a compliment to the angels rather than a slight.[4]

---

3. C.S. Lewis, *Preface to Paradise Lost* (London, 1942), 94.
4. Lewis, *Preface to Paradise Lost*, 94. Reference to Book V, 823-43.

Seen in this light, the reason for revolt, a "sense of injured merit" (I.98), encourages our laughter and puts Satanic thinking outside the realm of rationality as being neither fit to be taken seriously nor material worthy to be included in a justification of God's ways.[5] On the face of it the reader might ask, 'Is that all that evil is about?' The poet has to face the dilemma of either leaving the revolt in mystery, thus weakening his justification, his *reasoned* discourse, by allowing it to rest upon a mystery or, in attempting to explain the inexplicable, destroying the essential nature of the act of revolt, and in doing so, reduce the act in such a way that the series of responses which follow upon it do not need justification. He thus faces the possibility of attempting a justification where it is impossible (in the case of mystery), or providing one where none is needed. In either case, it is like trying to justify laughter, the Divine laughter of *Paradise Lost* which is on the one hand a mystery, impossible to justify, and on the other hand a non-rational act needing no justification.

This dilemma would stand had it not been for the condition of the reader. It is Man who seeks justification and Man to whom the justification is addressed, Man who partakes of the effects of the fruit of that forbidden tree. God's actions to himself do not need justification though he can and does provide justification. As the fallen angels cannot conceive of a justification of God's ways, so the good angels already have one, a justification strong enough to hold them against temptation and support them in battle against those who

---

5. Although God does laugh at Satan, showing that in itself Satan's predicament will be laughed at, the reader cannot as easily do so. He has to contend with his defect in hearing which the epic voice continually warns against. He has also to contend with the personal threat against Adam (and hence against himself) from Satan. Finally, Satan's predicament escapes being comic by being too near us. "A fallen man is very like a fallen angel." Lewis, 99.

would deny that justification. After Raphael has recounted to Adam the events that precede and lead up to Man's presence in the garden, adding a warning against transgression of God's sole command, Adam raises no question about God's goodness. Rather, he attributes glory "to the high / Creator" (VIII.12–13) and at the end is in a posture of adoration of God's "sovereign goodness" (VIII.647). Only after the fall, when he stands in the presence of his Judge, does Adam, recognizing his crime, seek to justify himself by laying the blame on the Woman:

> This woman whom thou madest to be my help,
> And gavest me as thy perfect gift, so good,
> So fit, so acceptable, so divine,
> That from her hand I could suspect no ill,
> And what she did, whatever in itself,
> Her doing seemed to justify the deed;

And after all of that merely to justify, he speaks plainly:

> She gave me of the tree, and I did eat (X.137–42).

The thrust of Adam's reply is not against the Woman but against the one who gave the Woman. In justifying himself, Adam is impugning God's goodness. It is where Adam justifies himself and blames God through his darkened intellect, and the darkness which he uses to hide his sin, that justification of God's ways to Man becomes relevant, even necessary.

It is to Adam then, in the agony and dread of his fallen condition, that a justification becomes necessary.[6]

---

6. Ostensibly in the epic, God's ways are being justified to Adam. In reality, God's ways are being justified to the reader who cries with Adam for an

> Ah, why should all mankind
> For one man's fault thus guiltless be condemned,
> If guiltless? (X.822–24).

> O why did God,
> Creator wise, that peopled highest heaven
> With spirits masculine, create at last
> This novelty on earth, this fair defect
> Of nature . . .? (X.888–92).

> O fleeting joys
> Of Paradise, dear bought with lasting woes!
> Did I request thee, maker, from my clay
> To mould me man . . .? (X.741–44).

The justification of God's ways to Man concerns three aspects of God: his justice, wisdom, and love. God's ways in justice are justified in Adam's eyes when he becomes convicted of his own guilt in transgressing God's law. They are further exonerated when Adam discovers the penalty of Death is more an act of mercy than of wrath. God's ways in wisdom are justified when Adam is brought to see that in all of Satan's arguments and machinations "There is no wisdom nor understanding nor counsel against the LORD."[7] God's

---

explanation. Stanley E. Fish points out that "Milton's purpose is to educate the reader to an awareness of his position and responsibilities as a fallen man, and to a sense of the distance which separates him from the innocence once his; his method is to make the reader "fall again exactly as Adam did and with Adam's troubled clarity, that is to say, 'not deceived'." *Surprised by Sin* (New York, 1967), 1.

7. *Proverbs 21:30* KJV.

ways in love are justified when Adam sees the good which God will bring out of evil:

> O goodness infinite, goodness immense!
> That all this good of evil shall produce,
> And evil turn to good; more wonderful
> Than that which by creation first brought forth
> Light out of darkness! full of doubt I stand,
> Whether I should repent me now of sin
> By me done and occasioned, or rejoice
> Much more, that much more good thereof shall spring
> (XII.469–76).

It is therefore in the end of evil rather than in its origin that any justification of it must be sought. If its origin is shrouded in mystery, its end is thoroughly manifest in the good that it brings about. There can be no justification for the existence of evil in itself, that is, in saying that evil serves its function by bringing more evil upon the head of him who exercises himself therein. In a God-centered universe, where all of creation is to serve the glory of God, his purpose will not be frustrated:

> Who seeks
> To lessen thee, against his purpose serves
> To manifest the more thy might: his evil
> Thou usest, and from thence createst more good
> (VII.613–16).

If Satan's self-contradiction presents us with sheer absurdity in itself, the outcome of that contradiction is not absurd in its relation to God's plan. Just as no creature was created unto itself but unto God, so the evil of any creature cannot exist unto itself but unto the good. The poet therefore escapes one horn of the dilemma in being able to include Satan's evil in the scheme of justifying God's ways to men by the very act of relating the evil to God's will. In itself, evil is non-rational and needs no justification; in relation to God's will, it provides occasion for creating more good. The poet also escapes the other horn of the dilemma by allowing evil in its origin to remain a mystery. Evil in itself is a mystery and no account can be given of it; in relation to God's will an account can be given of it. Since the poet is interested in justifying God's ways, he needs to be concerned with evil only in its relation to God, and in that relation, it only serves to bring about good. As it stands finally, Satan's evil in relation to a God-centered universe is self-contradictory, and to Satan in himself it brings self-deception and self-destruction whether he wills or not; Satan's evil in relation to God's will is self-contradictory, and to God and his creation it serves to bring about good whether he (Satan) wills or not.

It remains for us hereon to direct our attention to examining the action in the epic and to trace the process of Satan's activity to see where he intended it to bring him and where in fact it leads him—contrary to his expectations. The root of Satan's predicament lies in his attempt to maintain the doctrine that he is a self-existent being and not a creature. What brought him into this predicament we do not know. When all the rest of Heaven accepts the fact that they are God's creation, Satan only has doubted it, denied it rather, and asserted its opposite. Viewing himself and God as equally self-existent, he naturally desires to equal the Most High. He looks upon his attempt at the throne in Heaven as we would look upon an attempt of a *coup d'etat* here on earth. Satan's atheism and his resulting attempt at a military take-over in Heaven brings the reader to the action he finds at the opening of the epic.

Milton begins his epic with the falling action of Satan, an action which continues on the spiritual level throughout the epic at every turn of his uprising. The reader, approaching the work for the first time, does not feel the full impact of the fall until he reaches the last word: "arms."

> Him the almighty power
> Hurled headlong flaming from the ethereal sky
> With hideous ruin and combustion down
> To bottomless perdition, there to dwell
> In adamantine chains and penal fire,
> Who durst defy the omnipotent to arms (I.44–49).

The defiance of arms against Omnipotence crashes in its full force upon the reader's senses. Under the weight of the absurdity, the imagination staggers and collapses with the horrid crew on the floor of Hell. The imagination is stunned by the thought of such an attempt even as Satan and his crew are stunned by the result of such an attempt. The surprised reader has, as a result, been alerted; there is something unimaginably wrong with the fallen angels to have pitted arms against Omnipotence. The reader will seek to avoid the shock of falling into Hell again.[8] He will seek to prepare himself for what he will meet as he follows the action of Satan and his fallen host. From this point on, he is no longer an unsuspecting reader—his guard is up.

---

8. "What is your reaction when the second half of line 54 "for now the thought"— tells you that you are now with Satan in Hell? The unanimous reply is, 'surprise', and an involuntary question: "how did I come to be here?'" Fish, *Surprised by Sin*, 32–33.

The epic voice, juxtaposing the new scene of darkness against the memory of the light of Heaven, prepares the reader for Satan's surprise: "If thou beest he; but O how fallen! how changed" (I.84). This in turn, with the words "obdurate pride and steadfast hate" (I.58) still echoing in the reader's ear, quite naturally re-establish the hardening process: "yet not for those . . . do I repent or change" (I.94, 96). When everything else has changed, Satan's failure or refusal to change "that fixed mind" (I.97) would evoke admiration as of one who remains undaunted in the worst of circumstances. When, however, Satan raises again the issue of "dubious battle on the plains of heaven" (I.104), and of "the terror of this arm" (I.113) [his own] which made God "so late / Doubted his Empire" (I.113–4), he becomes merely a pathetic figure to the reader who remembers the vain attempt of arms against Omnipotence. The reader cannot be certain whether Satan knows he is lying or whether he has become victim of a self-imposed blindness. He has either fixed his mind because it is now too late to admit his mistake (what would happen to him in the eyes of those he has ruined?), or his mind is fixed because he can no longer face reality. In either case, the result is the same. "That fixed mind" (I.97) is fixed in self-contradictory rebellion. "That fixed mind" which he himself had fixed became "his doom" which "Reserved him to more wrath" (I.53–54).

"All is not lost" is true. "All is not lost" in Satan's mouth, however, is very poignant irony. Those very things which he considers not to be lost become the means of his losing everything:

> All is not lost; the unconquerable will,
> And study of revenge, immortal hate,
> And courage never to submit or yield (I.106–08).

The alternative to "the unconquerable will" does pass through his mind: "To bow and sue for grace / With suppliant knee . . ." (I.111–12). It is rejected because "that were low indeed, / That were an ignominy and shame beneath / This downfall" (I.114–16). The "obdurate pride" and "fixed mind" are taking effect. In ending his first speech, Satan appeals to "fate" (I.116) and "experience" (I.118) as the basis on which to base a "more successful hope" (I.120) in waging "by force or guile eternal war / Irreconcilable . . ." (I.121–22). And all of this is decided while he yet lies outstretched on the burning lake.

The epic voice re-entering corrects the reader's impression by keeping in his mind what he should know already. Satan gives the appearance of having regained full vigor, but Hell is a place of "lasting pain" (I.55) and there "hope never comes / That comes to all; but torture without end" (I.66–67). The description of the apostate Angel "in pain / Vaunting aloud, but racked with deep despair" (I.125–26) improves on the reader's view of Satan, not in a way that externally degrades him but in a way that is consistent with what has already been said and in a way that the reader is allowed to see him degenerate before his very eyes.[9] Satan must know what he feels in himself when he speaks of "more successful hope" (I.120). He must know that he is being untrue to himself, that his speech does not reflect the "deep despair" (I.126) he feels. What defines his degeneration is not merely that he is putting on an outward show but that he is going to act as if the show were true.

---

9. A.J. Waldock tries to argue the opposite: "It is a pretended exhibition of changes occurring: actually it is of the nature of an assertion that certain changes occur. The changes do not generate themselves from within: they are imposed from without. Satan in short, does not degenerate: he is degraded." *Paradise Lost and Its Critics* (Cambridge, 1947), 83.

His next step down comes in his reply to Beelzebub who suggests that the Almighty "Have left us this our spirit and strength entire / Strongly to . . . do him mightier service" (I.146–47, 149). To which "the arch-fiend" (I.156) replies that his mind is not only fixed but fixed to do evil. At every step down, Satan faces an alternative step upward which, in order to avoid, he must in a greater way involve himself in self-contradiction. He chooses the path of self-contradiction:

> But ever to do ill our sole delight,
> As being the contrary to his high will
> Whom we resist. If then his providence
> Out of our evil seek to bring forth good,
> Our labor must be to pervert that end (I.160–64).

Knowing that Providence seeks to bring good out of evil, he could frustrate Providence by producing no evil. Instead, he chooses to exert labor to pervert Providence—a sovereign will which by its nature cannot be turned aside. As the aim is contradictory in theory, so it is contradictory in reality. For the more evil that is used to overcome good, the more good it produces by being worked together for good.

The next move Satan makes is to get up off the fiery waves. For the first time, a description of his person is given in likening him to Leviathan, in size the greatest of all earthly creatures. The "arch-fiend" still lies "Chained on the burning lake" (I.209–10). The Almighty had intended him "there to dwell / In adamantine chains and penal fire" (I.47–48). Instead, he uses the respite from the "ministers of vengeance" (I.170) to violate God's judgment by throwing off his chains. The epic voice helps the reader to see that the chains were a means not so much of punishment as they were for restraining him from heaping on himself further damnation. Satan and his next mate rear themselves from off the lake, "Both glorying to have scaped the Stygian flood / As gods, and by their own recovered strength, / Not by the sufferance of supernal power" (I.239–41).[10] The glorying is in mere appearances, however, for Satan would have remained on the lake:

> nor ever thence
> Had risen or heaved his head, but that the will
> And high permission of all-ruling heaven
> Left him at large to his own dark designs,
> That with reiterated crimes he might
> Heap on himself damnation, while he sought
> Evil to others, and enraged might see
> How all his malice served but to bring forth
> Infinite goodness, grace and mercy shown
> On man by him seduced, but on himself
> Treble confusion, wrath and vengeance poured (I.210–20).

Persisting in his self-contradictory rebellion, Satan must deceive himself into thinking that the divine will can be withstood. Rebellion co-exists with but is, in Satan's case, logically prior to deception; rebellion cuts off any real consideration of the nature of the divine will and seeks justification in appearances.[11]

---

10. Milton's reference to "Supernal Power" instead of "Permissive Will" is in accord with the Thomistic view of free will which holds that while the will in every rational being is free to choose, the power of the will to act depends on grace from the creator who sustains his universe. M.D. Knowles, *The Nature of Mysticism* (New York, 1966), 20.

11. Since he invariably knows what the alternatives are before choosing, his deception (as means) must follow his choosing which establishes him in a

More deliberations and accusations follow before he determines that it is "Better to reign in hell, than serve in heaven" (I.263). Rejecting the alternative of serving in Heaven he becomes caught in the trap of leadership. Satan does not reject serving in Heaven but serving anywhere. To fulfill his ambition to rule, he must have a multitude over which to rule. To that selfish end, he raises the host over which he is to reign and by which he seeks to extenuate his own glory. But in raising them he is calling up doom upon his own head. The simile describing the act bears this out. The likening of the host of fallen angels to "a pitchy cloud / Of locusts, warping on the eastern wind, / That over the realm of impious Pharaoh hung" (I.340–42) enables the reader to see the comparison between the devils and Satan on the one hand, and the locusts and Pharaoh on the other hand. As the locusts were raised against Pharaoh, so the devils are being raised by Satan against himself. And the reader is expected to know that Pharaoh in Biblical narrative is a type of Satan.

Following upon the catalogue of demons, the parade of the fallen host, and the military review, Satan, himself an outward show, glories. His heart now distends with pride and hardens:

> but his face
> Deep scars of thunder had intrenched, and care
> Sat on his faded cheek, but under brows
> Of dauntless courage, and considerate pride
> Waiting revenge (I.600–04).

---

self-contradictory end. Again, since he is deceived in the appearance that he can get up from the lake in his own strength and since his getting up follows his will to get up, his deception follows his rebellion or self-contradiction.

He who would not change his "fixed mind" (I.97) has already moved from open war (I.49), to subversion (I.164), to harassment (I.188), and now to revenge. The address to his troops (the first after their fall), intending to inspire new confidence, succeeds. But apart from the usual lies, vilification, and empty rhetoric, it reveals essentially that the work against Heaven is to continue, preferably by fraud and guile "that he no less / At length from us may find, who overcomes / By force, hath overcome but half his foe" (I.647–49). God, by whose will Satan is allowed to rise from the lake to plot more rebellion, is to be taken by surprise by that plotting. Satan thus falls another grade lower. And when the reader for the first time hears that perhaps the revenge on God will be directed toward Man, Satan falls again. Satan's character encompasses a villany that the reader had thought was not possible. Since he cannot hurt God directly, he can always vent his spleen on—Man. Simple.

The resolution ending the speech calls for war: "War then, war / Open or understood..." (I.661–62). Accompanying this resolve, as usual, is an alternative which has been rejected. "Peace is despaired, / For who can think submission?" (I.660–61). Peace is not despaired because God will not accept a reconciliation. His foreknowledge, by which he acts, knew that Satan would refuse to consider submission. If God's acts make no room for reconciliation, it is not by his will but by his foreknowledge, which has no effect on determining the choices which it knows will be made. Thus Satan, driving himself further from God, becomes more entangled in self-contradiction. Rejecting the alternative, he must now seek a way to proceed in self-contradiction, and that way is the way of self-delusion.

From the beginning of the epic, the reader is told that Satan sought to raise himself above his peers, enlisting their own support (unwittingly) for this purpose. The attempt to rise above his peers is necessitated by Satan's desire to be like the Most High who reigns over a host. Satan's action is not directed toward the general good but a personal end.

In other words, denying the fallen angels as his peers, they become pawns for his ambition. They provide him with an army against God, with consolation in his fall, "Innumerable force of spirits armed / That durst dislike his reign, and me preferring" (I.101–02). They also serve as the host over which he can reign. But to deny service to God and render it to Satan will appear senseless to the fallen angels. This would mean that he is not only equal to but greater than God. Satan wants equality with God. To get that he must make everyone equal. But he does not want the other angels to be equal with himself because he wants to rule over them. The self-contradiction requires him to make the angels feel equal while establishing his superiority and his right to reign over them. Satan must provide sufficient camouflage to hide the real issue.

The reader can detect the camouflage in the appearance of equality that Satan gives to his associates: "mutual league / United thoughts . . . equal hope / . . . equal ruin" (I.87–88, 91). Equality as peers is never admitted. Although equality allows for leadership among peers, Satan is not trying to achieve leadership. He already has it by hierarchy. In seeking to be like the Most High, he is seeking to have rule over his peers. This elicited the utterance, "Better to reign in hell, than serve in heaven" (I.263). Leadership and ruling must be viewed as distinct in the context of the epic. Hierarchy which was established by sovereign will according to the different kinds God created, and not according to merit, is viewed by Satan as old custom. In denying God's right to rule by hierarchy, Satan denies also his right to leadership by hierarchy. But because of his ambition to *rule* where lack of hierarchy makes nonsense of the concept of ruling, he is caught in a double contradiction. He must find some other means for hierarchy than God's will. Since there is no other means, he deludes himself into finding one—merit. His telltale reference to "injured merit" (I.98) and his condemnation of God's rule by "old repute, / Consent or custom" (I.639–640) requires him to establish his rule by merit. But merit among peers never justifies essential elevation above peers; it only serves to cloud the issue of real hierarchy and real equality.[12] Again, Satan provides the fallen spirits with a sense of equality by allowing decisions to appear to be made by a council whereas, in fact, he has already more than suggested what the next move will be. Content with generous showing of Satan's democratic process, the Hellish crew falls to its task of constructing Pandemonium, the capitol seat of Hell's godlike imitate kingdom and the archetype of the kingdoms of this world.

With the council called together in Book II, the reader, who remembers Satan's earlier resolution of immortal hate toward God and his determination to "pursue / Vain war with heaven" (II.8–9) by fraud or guile, may wonder now what will happen in the council if the council fails to adopt his plan. He may further wonder at the threat posed to Satan's reign by open debate in the council. Yet it was Satan who suggested the meeting of the council.

Somehow Satan must cause his plan to be approved and in such a way that he succeeds in his ambition to reign. As Satan opens the council, the reader sees the result of his self-contradictory aspiration. After a few remarks to stir up hope in his audience, he proceeds to use the council

---

12. In Book III (290–315) where mention is made of merit twice, we find in the first instance that it is the merit of Christ imputed to the sinner. In the second instance we find that Messiah is regaining by merit his birth-right which, as the Son of God, he had quitted in becoming Flesh. In neither instance is there the implication that merit advances one in God's hierarchy.

to fulfill his ambition. He begins to outline his reasons for having rule over them:

> Me though just right, and the fixed laws of heaven
> Did first create your leader, next free choice,
> With what besides, in counsel or in fight,
> Hath been achieved of merit, yet this loss
> Thus far at least recovered, hath much more
> Established in a safe unenvied throne
> Yielded with full consent (II.18–24).

Having sought to overthrow rule in Heaven, he must now justify it in Hell. The first appeal, to "fixed laws of heaven" (II.18) which had given him leadership, the reader will recognize as an appeal to hierarchy which in Heaven he had rejected. The second appeal to "free choice" (II.19) is left up in the air. The reader cannot tell whose choice he is referring to, his own or his followers. Choosing himself to be their leader is ludicrous; that they had chosen him is contrary to their avowed purpose of fighting for equality and liberty. The second appeal is unsupportable either way, probably accounting for its mere mention and ambiguity. The next appeal to merit is pure emptiness. His advice, when followed, led to revolt and a war disastrous to their eternal happiness. For this, he argues that he merits being their leader. Last of all, he boasts of the stability of Hell's throne. It is so bad to be Hell's emperor, no one will envy you. It entails so much danger that the position will be gladly yielded up. No one is ambitious enough to covet more pain. This, however, does not restrain Satan from nominating himself candidate for the post.

Since Satan earnestly covets Hell's throne, and since he believes that he in truth is worthy of it, the reader must assume that Satan feels he is speaking the truth. The fact that every one of his appeals are reasons for him not to receive or assume the throne clues the reader to the disintegration of Satan's thinking. The disintegration is greater than before because he has greater access to knowing the truth of what he has said. He could plead ignorance of God's might, but he cannot plead ignorance of what he himself has done. When he argues that experience has advanced foresight (I.119), he is both right and wrong. Foresight keeps them from again trying arms against God, but it does not teach them not to use guile. When Satan argues that the stability of Hell's throne is a great advantage, assuring their prosperity, he is totally wrong. For every prosperity undermines the stability of the throne by increasing the good in it to be envied, and every decrease in stability decreases its advantage. Hell is not only, as Charles Williams puts it, "inaccurate;" it is self-contradictory.

The debate in Hell provides the reader with interesting foils to Satan. Moloch counsels suicidal war, thinking nothing can be worse than to sit "lingering here" (II.56). Belial counsels "peaceful sloth" (II.227), neither wanting to be driven to "flat despair" (II.143) by a second war nor to keep alive the agonizing memory of their former state. "Is this then worst . . .?" (II.163). Belial also reckons with the reality that guile is useless against God who "All these our motions vain, sees and derides" (II.191). Mammon's persuasion is that they make Hell a substitute for Heaven: "Nor want we skill or art, from whence to raise / Magnificence; and what can heaven show more?" (II.272–273). Beelzebub, who up to now has only appeared as the flatterer, echoing the master's lies, reiterates what Satan had earlier proposed. An attempt by force or guile against God's new creation, Man, would "surpass / Common revenge, and interrupt his joy / In our confusion, and our Joy upraise / In his disturbance"

(II.370–73). Such deep malice was beyond the power of the other demons to suggest, but once plainly expressed, they found in that bold design fulfillment of their own inclinations. Arms and guile may still be employed; peaceful sloth may still be had; new empires may be gained without giving up "obdurate pride and steadfast hate" (I.58).

Well pleased with the success of his plan, Satan presses on to establish his rule. They must now decide who first will undertake that dangerous expedition. The dramatic moment is at hand. Satan describes the hazards and terrors that the journey necessitates, awaiting with "look suspense . . . who appeared / To second, or oppose, or undertake / The perilous attempt" (II.418–20). Terrified into silence, no one was found "So hardy as to proffer or accept / Alone the dreadful voyage" (II.425–26). Assured of no rivalry, Satan evokes even greater terrors in their minds, designed to increase his own merit. For now he, for their general safety, would despise his own. The greater the difficulty he has proposed, the further he may raise himself above them:

> But I should ill become this throne, O peers,
> And this imperial sovereignty, adorned
> With splendor, armed with power, if aught proposed
> And judged of public moment, in the shape
> Of difficulty or danger could deter
> Me from attempting (II.445–50).

Certain now of achieving the throne, he grants to them the empty title of "peers," going on to praise his own "imperial sovereignty" (II.446) and "assume / These royalties" (II.450–451) before their very eyes. No sooner having done, he issues his first command, not as General but as the Saviour-King. "Go therefore . . . render hell / More tolerable ... intermit no watch ... while I abroad / Through all the coasts of dark destruction seek / Deliverance for us all" (II.456, 459–60, 462–65).

Merit is, by its nature, so relative, so inviting to competition, that it must be maintained by greater and greater exploits or by avoiding challenges. Satan secures his merit by avoiding challenges: "this enterprise / None shall partake with me" (II.465–66). Rising, he prevents all replies or new offers from others among the chief which, certain to be refused, "might in opinion stand / His rivals, winning cheap the high repute / Which he through hazard huge must earn" (II.471–73). The effect of his assumption of command is already felt. They do not dread the journey more than they fear his forbidding voice; "this enterprise / None shall partake with me" (II.465–66). His bid for power achieves complete dramatic success when:

> Towards him they bend
> With awful reverence prone; and as a god
> Extol him equal to the highest in heaven (II.477–79).

As "hell's dread emperor with pomp supreme, / And Godlike imitated state" (II.510–11), and with "A globe of fiery seraphim" (II.512) enclosing him round, Satan's aspiration to rise above his peers and equal the Most High is fulfilled.

Hell's parody of Heaven goes a step further in the episode following the council's dispersal. Seeking his way out of Hell, Satan reaches the bounds of Hell, and at the gate of Hell, confronts on either side a "formidable shape" (II.649). To the one approaching with a threatening dart preventing his way, Satan flashes out, "Whence and what art thou, execrable shape" (II.681). The reader is surprised by the accuracy and fearlessness of the reply, wondering who the new combatant might be that thus, against Satan's head, would level his deadly aim. Like Satan, the reader is totally unprepared to hear these "shapes" own Satan as their progenitor. Satan's denial is most revealing. "I know thee not, nor ever saw till now / Sight more detestable than him and thee" (II.744–45). The "snaky sorceress" (II.724) reminds him of how she had sprung forth shining heavenly fair and full grown from his head, "when at the assembly, and in sight / Of all the Seraphim with thee combined / In bold conspiracy against heaven's king, / All on a sudden miserable pain / Surprised thee . . ." (II.749–53). Called Sin by the Seraphim, she had, "with attractive graces" (II.762), enticed Satan who beheld in her his perfect image. She bore progeny to Satan, Death the dart-bearer, and was with the rebels cast out of Heaven, having been given the key to Hell's gate that only by Sin could one get in or out of Hell.

The reader will have recognized in Satan, Sin, and Death, Hell's counterpart to the Father, the Son, and the Holy Spirit.[13] He will also have recognized the source of the allegory: "every man is tempted when he is drawn away of his own lust and enticed. Then when lust hath conceived, it bringeth forth sin: and sin when it is finished bringeth forth death."[14] Satan, who had been enticed by his lust for glory, willingly entered into the revolt against God. In the midst of the assembly, while conspiring against God, his lust was fully ripened. Then, whether he would or not, revolt tore itself from his head in the form of Sin. Enamored by his "perfect image" (II.764), Sin conceived and brought forth Death. What Satan once recognized as his perfect image has now become a most detestable sight. Before venturing

---

13. A perfect parallel is present. As the Son is begotten of the Father, so Sin was begotten of Satan; as the Holy Spirit proceeds from the Father through the Son, so Death proceeds from Satan through Sin.

14. *James 1:14–15* KJV.

out on his mission against creatures innocent of any harm toward him, Satan is brought to see in his perfect image, Sin, what he has become. And as he stands ready at Hell's gate to pursue vain war with Heaven, the fruit of his sin, Death, stands ready to redound upon his own head. His failure to recognize his offspring, Sin and Death, reflects the depths of spiritual blindness to which he had fallen; his detestation of them is a detestation of himself. Sin, which in Heaven was pleasurable for a season, has become to him in Hell detestable for eternity.

But the fact that God had committed the key of Hell's gate to Sin was tantamount to putting the power of opening the gate in Satan's own power. Presumably, Satan would recognize the detestable nature of that which would open the gate to him and turn from it. Simply by his act of sin, he will get out, just as man by his act of sin will get in. The personified warning in Sin of what that act would be like is no deterrence to Satan. Neither is there deterrence from sin in the personified fruit of sin, Death, which threatens to redound on his own head. At this decisive step forward, Satan is faced with a dire warning against his persistence in sin. He chooses to neglect that warning at the cost of further abandonment of his true being.[15] Those shapes that were to him truly disgusting he now calls "Dear daughter . . . And my fair Son" (II.817–18). Sin, in its most apparent and detestable form, unlocks the gate of Hell to him.

The reader who has followed Satan's journey across the realm of Chaos and Night to the outermost limit of God's new creation is, in Book II, brought to the place of Heavenly vision and made to hear the secret counsels

---

15. T. Kranidas in his book *The Fierce Equation* (London, 1965), points out that "Disguise and its implication about the sacrifice of total self, is implicit in the Satan of Books I and II and subtly developed and enlarged throughout the poem until the last climactic transformation of Book X." p. 125.

of the Godhead. He is informed about the outcome of Satan's adventure against Man, about the operations of free will, foreknowledge, divine justice, and grace. He draws the contrast between the Heavenly and Hellish councils. In Heaven's "where shall we find such love"?[16] (to redeem Man), he hears Hell's echo, 'where shall we find such hate?' (to ruin Man). He puts side by side the Son becoming Man to save Man, and Satan becoming 'God' to destroy Man; the Son's yielding to Death's dart unto ultimate victory, and Satan's circumventing Death's dart unto ultimate defeat. The reader becomes increasingly aware of the absolute difference between Heaven and Hell, in spite of Hell's attempt to form a "Godlike imitated state" (II.511). He also sees that Hell is not only contradictory to Heaven but contradictory to itself and that on the grandest scale.

If it has been equivocal up to this point whether Satan is lying or blind in what he says, the episodes which bring him to the seat of Man remove all doubt. Vulture-like, the Fiend scans the new worlds, "bent on his prey" (III.441). "The golden sun in splendor likest heaven / Allured his eye" (III.572–573). This place, "beyond expression bright" (III.591), becomes the scene of another step toward total internal darkness. For here it is that Satan, on finding the Archangel Uriel, discovers himself to the Angel in the form of "a stripling Cherub" (III.636), seeking his way to the seat of Man to behold and wonder at God's new creation. The step forward in his dark design requires him to take another step backward in losing his original identity. In order to gain the direction he needs to take his next step, he has to use disguise: a lie on a conscious level. He must also practice self-contradiction as an art, the art of appearing what one is

---

16. Book III (213).

not—hypocrisy. In order to get the Angel's help, he feigns praise to the great Creator:

> Who justly hath driven out his rebel foes
> To deepest hell, and to repair that loss
> Created this new happy race of men
> To serve him better: wise are all his ways (III.677–80).

It may be questioned whether Satan's desire to make his real position invisible stems from the fact that he is talking to an enemy who cannot be persuaded, or because his real position is too self-contradictory to be able to persuade anyone. That he used persuasion in Hell is obvious. That he does not use it here reflects the fact that he cannot admit a noble motive. Perhaps fighting against God for the cause of Liberty, however misconstrued, still has its splendor, though fallen. To wreak vengeance on innocent Man has no splendor. Satan's disguise is not a military tactic; it is, as the epic voice calls it, hypocrisy, representing a further decline in his moral stature.

The unfolding of the Satanic character reaches its height when he, now in prospect of Eden, "Begins his dire attempt" (IV.15). As he comes closest to repeating his crime, closest therefore in his return to the scene of his crime (in an internal sense),[17] he experiences tumultuous upheavals in his breast. The glory of the new world, reminiscent of Heaven's glory, awakens conscience, which wakens despair. Recollecting what he once was, what is, and what must be, he attempts to understand what moved him from his

---

17. Here I am comparing the seduction of the angels and the seduction of Man. The actual place is different but the crime itself of seduction is strikingly similar even though the former seduction occurred in a manner refutable (eg., by Abdiel), while the latter occurred in a disguise not penetrable.

first state. Each reason he suggests he himself rejects. He is completely honest since there is no one present to whom he must adjust himself. Finding the source of his rebellion only in himself, he curses himself, realizing finally:

> Which way I fly is hell; myself am hell;
> And in the lowest deep a lower deep
> Still threatening to devour me opens wide,
> To which the hell I suffer seems a heaven (IV.75–78).

For the first time in the poem, the self-contradiction in thought is broken only in discovering that there is a self-contradiction in being.[18] The possibility of changing that being through repentance is considered: "But say I could repent . . .?" (IV.93). The truth is that he cannot repent because he is unable to conceive of true repentance. He only gets to "feigned submission . . . made in pain" (IV.96–97), leading eventually to a worse relapse and heavier fall. He argues that true reconciliation can never grow "Where wounds of deadly hate have pierced so deep" (IV.99). The reader, however, does not recall any hate from Heaven. He recalls only that Satan's rebellion will redound on his own head. He recalls also that Satan has fixed his mind in "steadfast hate" (I.58). Satan's desire has been granted to him. He wanted to hate always. Now, whether he wills or not, he cannot avoid hating. Long ago, he had bid farewell

---

18. Merritt Y. Hughes in his article "Myself am Hell" provides an excellent substantiation of the view that for Milton the Hell of mind is more fundamental than the Hell of place and that the former is inescapable even as Lethe, the river of Oblivion, is unattainable. *Ten Perspectives on Milton* (Yale University Press, 1965), 145. By the Hell of mind or the sophisticated idea of Hell, as Hughes calls it, is probably meant what I mean by the Hell of being. Satan may remove the self-contradiction which denies his basic self-contradiction but he cannot remove the basic self-contradiction.

to his hope. What seems to Satan his climactic choice, "Evil be thou my good," merely reiterates what he had said in Book I: "But ever to do ill our sole delight, / As being the contrary to his high will" (160–61). The only difference here is that he makes this choice after a thoroughly correct understanding of himself and his situation.

For the rest of his appearance in the epic, Satan does not make any real choices. He has been facing his only real choice—that of submission—in more and more explicit ways, each time choosing the way of evil more explicitly. Here the most explicit choice of evil is followed, while he speaks, by a singular diminishing of his outward glory, "Thrice changed with pale, ire, envy and despair, / Which marred his borrowed visage" (IV.115–16). The steady decline in all of his energies is interrupted only by Rachel's depiction of him in Heaven before his fall. Satan appears more and more like the Devil of popular imagination rather than the Prince of Hell. Now he is the "prowling wolf" (IV.183), "a thief bent to unhoard the cash" (IV.188), and the Cormorant "on the tree of life" (IV.194). All delights serve only to increase his misery (IV.286), and at the sight of the First Pair in their happy state, he explodes, "O hell!" (IV.358). He "could love" (IV.363), "could pity" (IV.374) the human pair, but "conquering this new world, compels me now / To do what else though damned I should abhor" (IV.391–2). Outside the privacy of their conjugal bower, he becomes a mere peeping Tom who, for envy, turns aside, "yet with jealous leer malign" (IV.503) eyes them askance. The disguise begun as a stripling Cherub is finally uncovered when, in the form of a toad at the ear of Eve, Satan is surprised by the youthful angels on patrol.

Resuming his own shape, the Fiend is abashed to learn that so much was his luster "visibly impaired" (IV.850) he is scarcely recognizable. His scornful "Know ye not me?"

(IV.828) carries with it a tinge of panic over lost identity. To Gabriel, his contemptuous "Lives there who loves his pain?" (IV.888) carries with it a plea for sympathy. Stung by Gabriel's bright sarcasm, "Courageous chief, / The first in flight from pain" (IV.920–21), Satan replies in effect, 'I'm not afraid of you.' The illimitable excitement of battle grips the angelic squadron. "To say and straight unsay" (IV.947). Gabriel catches Satan between his lie, flying-pain, and his half-truth, faithful-leader-on-spying-mission. The air brisks for the horrid fray. The battle is prevented only by the Eternal whose celestial scale shows Satan how wanting he would be if he refuses to leave. Satan flees.

In the next four books of the epic consisting of the education of Adam, the reader is informed of the events in Heaven which led up to Satan's revolt. The almighty Father decreed that the Son shall be the head of all the Heavenly hierarchy. Disobedience to the Son will constitute disobedience to God, resulting in everlasting separation from God. Moved with envy, pride, and malice against the Son of God, Satan withdrew his hosts from among the assembled spirits to prepare "fit entertainment" (V.690) for the new King. The presence of evil in Satan in the midst of Heavenly beatitude is not as startling to the reader as it might be because the reader has already followed his career of evil since his fall from Heaven. Furthermore, he has had an accurate recapitulation and analysis of the fall from Satan's own mouth (IV.32–113). There the reader hears Satan acknowledge that he is a creature whom "he created what I was / In that bright eminence" (IV.43–44). Here Satan justifies his resistance to God's decree by claiming equality and/or freedom for all spirits, denying that they are creatures:

> Will ye submit your necks, and choose to bend
> The supple knee? Ye will not, if I trust
> To know ye right, or if ye know yourselves
> Natives and sons of heaven possessed before
> By none, and if not equal all, yet free,
> Equally free . . . (V.787–92).

With "calumnious art" (V.770), he summarizes the intention of his speech: "not to serve!" (V.802).

Point for point, Abdiel answers his charge. The most telling part of the reply is Abdiel's question: "Thyself . . . dost thou count . . . Equal to him begotten son, by whom . . . the mighty Father made / All things, even thee . . .?" (V.833, 835–37). Satan's reply is scarcely more than boring. He claims on the one hand to be *sui generis,* admitting in the same breath ignorance of his beginning, and on the other hand to have sprung up by "fatal course" (V.861), the result of a fixed power outside of himself. Satan's rejection of a Creator-God, creation by the Son, and the deity of the Son are aimed more at Messiah than at the Father. In the chronology of eternity, Satan's revolt came after the Son was begotten. The temptation is to ask whether Satan would have revolted if God had not made the decree concerning his Son. Is the mystery of iniquity then bound up with Satan's failure to comprehend the mystery of the Trinity? Or is there no causal connection between Satan's knowledge and his sin? Is the relation between righteousness and truth and evil and error merely a contingent one or is it a necessary one? Is it necessary in both cases or is it only in the first case and not the second? If sin cannot be justified by any knowledge, why is an appeal to knowledge always used in its justification or in its refutation (both Satan and Abdiel use arguments to support their positions)?

Unless sin is viewed as disobedience to God's will, no headway can be made in understanding Milton's account of Satan's fall. In the divine economy, God's will is based on knowledge but knowledge which is inscrutable.[19] Thus, while God's decree that the Son shall reign is based on knowledge (or on reality, which has its source in God himself), the decree itself is not a knowledge claim. Any refutation of the rational ground of that Will is futile since God "useth knowledge aright."[20] Refutation may only be attempted against the sovereignty of that Will or the right of that Will to issue orders. Satan's argument attempted to refute the right of that Will by denying the basis of that right, God's (and hence Messiah's) position as Creator. Abdiel argues for both the right of that Will, "by right endued / With regal sceptre" (V.815–16), and the rational basis of that Will: "shalt thou dispute / With him the points of liberty . . .?" (V.822–23). Since God's command requires a choice and not argument, Satan's use of argument is merely a cover-up for his disobedience. Satan is not merely blind or lying but deceiving himself if he thinks he is acting on the basis of knowledge without any choice involved. Like all creatures, Satan just finds himself existing without knowing how or why. If he claims to act on the basis of knowledge, his ignorance which is non-knowledge can consistently be followed only by non-action. Any action therefore must be preceded by a choice of what he will believe. Satan chooses to deny that he is a creature. His choice is, of course, wrong, having no basis in reality. He deceives himself in thinking that he does not make a choice, that his conclusion is forced

---

19. The question whether God's will or God's intelligence is more fundamental is not at issue. Whether in fact the question is a meaningful one I have no way of knowing. But that in Milton's frame of reference God's will is inscrutable is readily attested to by the content of the Book of Job.

20. *Proverbs 15:2* KJV.

upon him by reason, and that his revolt must follow as a matter of course from his conclusion. In choosing what he will believe, Satan, in the strongest terms, chooses to disobey. Thus his act of rebellion and his self-deception is one and the same act. The causal connection between knowledge and sin disappears because cause and effect cannot be separated, either ontologically or empirically, from each other. Thus, Satan's fall is not due to an error of judgment which may be corrected by knowing the truth, but to an error of will which determines the truth for him, a truth which is self-contradictory in both thought and reality. The battle in Heaven and the results which follow upon it are merely outward manifestations of his internal self-contradiction.

In Book IX, the reader finds that Satan has returned to the garden in the form of mist, his way being increasingly straitened by "the hateful siege / Of contraries" (IX.121–22). All good to him becomes bane and only in destroying does he find ease for his relentless thoughts. Dreading the vigilance of the angelic watch, he considers every creature, seeking which might most aptly serve to hide him and his dark intent:

> Him after long debate, irresolute
> Of thoughts revolved, his final sentence chose
> Fit vessel . . . (IX.87–89).

He chooses the serpent. The *double entendre* of "sentence" in "his final sentence chose" (IX.88) points to the culmination of the Satanic career. As he chose his self-deception in Heaven, he here chooses the deformation of his being, not however without realizing the immediate implication of that "foul descent":

> But what will not ambition and revenge
> Descend to? Who aspires must down as low
> As high he soared, obnoxious first or last
> To basest things. Revenge, at first though sweet,
> Better ere long back on itself recoils;
> Let it . . . (IX.168–73).

In the temptation of Eve, Satan is trying to involve her in what he has involved himself—rebellion. The temptation scene thus becomes a reenactment of Satan's fall. That he uses disguise and lies to persuade her to his own position reflects an interesting metamorphosis in Satan. He has ceased being a liar and has become a Lie. As a liar, he believes he is outside of his lie. As a Lie, he knows that he embodies his lies. If he did not know he embodied his own lies, that would merely be blindness. But here he knows that he is lying and that he embodies his lies. In reproducing his fall in Eve, he is forced to use the same arguments he used on himself. Only then he thought they were true; now he knows they are false. He argues that God's law impairs their freedom (IX.656); he urges her not to believe "those rigid threats of death" (IX.685); he points out that by venturing higher than his lot, he has attained a life more perfect "than fate / Meant me" (IX.689–90); he urges her to learn by experience (IX.699). Because he has become a Lie, only lies can be used to support his position, just as only truth can be used to support the Truth. Satan is not only a liar but the Father of lies, being himself like unto what he begets.

The human pair having fallen, the Son of God descends to pass judgment on Satan and on Adam and Eve. Not discerning that the curse on the Serpent is directed toward him, Satan, "With joy / And tidings fraught" (Book X,

345–46), returns to Hell. His sudden re-appearance on the throne of Hell heightens the effect of his annunciation:

> him by fraud I have seduced
> From his creator . . . (X.485–86).

And merely glossing over his own judgment, he ends his account:

> But up now and enter into full bliss (X.503).

The reader, like Satan, has been preparing himself for this moment:

> So having said, a while he stood, expecting
> Their universal shout and high applause
> To fill his ear, when contrary he hears
> On all sides, from innumerable tongues
> A dismal universal hiss, the sound
> Of public scorn; he wondered, but not long
> Had leisure, wondering at himself now more;
> His visage drawn he felt to sharp and spare,
> His arms clung to his ribs, his legs entwining
> Each other, till supplanted down he fell
> A monstrous serpent on his belly prone,
> Reluctant, but in vain, a greater power
> Now ruled him, punished in the shape he sinned,
> According to his doom: he would have spoke,
> But hiss for hiss returned with forked tongue
> To forked tongue, for now were all transformed
> Alike, to serpents all as accessories (X.504–20).

Amazement seizes the reader at the dramatic reversal. On him astonishment falls as horror fell on the spirits waiting in the field outside. The exploding hiss turns into a cascading action as the serpents pour out into the open field and into "A grove hard by, sprung up with this their change" (X.548). All the trees of the grove are "laden with fair fruit, like that / Which grew in Paradise, the bait of Eve / Used by the tempter" (X.550–52). Driven by hunger and thirst, the serpents bite into the fruits, finding instead of delectable juice, that they chewed bitter ashes. Yet not for that did they cease. Again and again, they bite, being filled repeatedly with soot and cinders. Relief comes to the reader as the epic voice shifts the scene from the frustrating present to the protracted future. The plague and famine and ceaseless hiss of the serpents will return yearly. The spirits are "to undergo / This annual humbling certain numbered days, / To dash their pride, and joy for man seduced" (X.575–77).

"For man seduced." The reader's attention turns from the distant future, into which the Satanic career has faded, and reconsiders Satan's reversal with a more collected mind. The fall from the throne in the form of a serpent represents Satan's second fall. From voluntary disguise as a serpent, he has been changed to a serpent in reality, whether he wills or not. From deceiver to deceived, from supplanter to supplanted, from highest Heaven to lowest Hell—such is the contradictoriness of sin. Yet it was his own doing which redounded upon his head. He chose "that fixed mind" (I.97). He chose evil for his good. He chose the form "which of all / Most opportune might serve his wiles" (IX.84–5). In every instance, Satan's desire has been granted—ironically.

APPENDICES

Appendix A

EXISTENTIAL HERMENEUTICS
Prolegomena to Philosophy of Art

THE NATURE OF INTERPRETATION

WE INTERPRET (GIVE MEANING TO) our experience in light of who we are: one's presupposition, personality, background, and mood. No experience is meaningful without interpretation: no sensory, personal, or cultural experience in art, literature, or history.

There are two sets of contradictory basic beliefs; both cannot be true, and both cannot be false. One's set of basic beliefs constitutes a worldview, which is the foundation for culture.[1] *In epistemology,* basic things (about God and man and good and evil) are clear to reason (the Principle of Clarity), vs. basic things are not clear (skepticism and fideism).[2] *In metaphysics,* only some is eternal (theism) vs. all or none is eternal (non-theism). *In ethics,* the good is the end in itself (teleology), not virtue (which is the means to the good) or happiness (which is the effect of possessing

---

1. Gangadean, "Paper No. 19: Foundation for Philosophy of History," in *The Logos Papers*, 123–125.
2. Gangadean, *Philosophical Foundation*, 3–5, 287–292; Gangadean, *The Westminster Confession,* 1–13; Gangadean, "Paper No. 53: Common Ground (Part IV)," in *The Logos Papers*, 283–286.

what is the good) vs. virtue is the good (deontology) or happiness is the good (hedonism).

We are more or less conscious and consistent in holding our basic beliefs. Unbelief remains in the believer, and belief remains in the unbeliever. We should be more conscious and consistent; we should be concerned with consistency; we should have integrity, which is unity in thought, word, and deed.[3] Everyone has an admixture of both sets, one set being existentially more basic than the other. Personal and corporate history is an outworking of the conflict of basic beliefs in each person and in each group of persons. The degree of one's consciousness and consistency in basic belief depends on one's personality focus, whether intellectual, emotional, or practical; developmental factors inform one's intellectual background, and one's spiritual mood reflects existential consistency.

Only the worldview/presupposition that retains meaning will last. Persons and cultures naturally move further into the meaningfulness of life or the meaninglessness of death. Words are conventional signs used to express thoughts (concepts, judgments, and arguments). The same words used in different worldviews are worlds apart in meaning or the lack thereof.

THE NATURE OF MAN AND THE KNOWLEDGE OF GOD THROUGH THE WORK OF DOMINION

It is self-evident that man is a rational animal. The good for man, as a rational being, is the use of reason to the fullest. Since reason is used to grasp the nature of things, the good for man as a rational being is to understand the

---

3. Gangadean, *Philosophical Foundation*, 199–205.

nature of things. Since the nature of things reveal the nature of the Creator, good for man is the knowledge of God.[4] The chief end of man is the end in itself, the highest good, which is eternal life, the knowledge of God. Man is made in the image of God,[5] to know God through the work of dominion, to fill the earth with the knowledge of God as the waters cover the sea.[6]

In dominion, man is to name the creation, which reveals God's glory, and to rule over it. *Naming* is by grasping the essence of things created. *Ruling* is by developing the powers latent in himself and the creation. Naming precedes ruling; essence precedes function. Dominion extends to the natural and human realms. In nature, under natural law, through science by naming (definitions, principles, and laws) and technology by ruling (applications, inventions, and innovations). Human beings under the moral law, rule through the Humanities. The Humanities answer the question, "What is Man?" by examining man's view of himself in the varying worldviews and cultures. The Humanities name human nature, while the Arts develop the powers within man through communication.

---

4. Gangadean, *Philosophical Foundation*, 171–177, 208–211; Surrendra Gangadean, *The Westminster Shorter and Larger Catechisms: A Doxological Understanding* (Phoenix: Logos Papers Press, 2023), 109–111, 321–325; Gangadean, *On Natural and Revealed Theology*, 33–39, 127–139.

5. Surrendra Gangadean, *The Biblical Worldview: Creation, Fall, Redemption. Genesis 1–3: Scripture in Organic Seed Form* (Phoenix: Logos Papers Press, 2024), 109–124; Gangadean, *The Westminster Confession*, 79–83; Gangadean, *The Westminster Catechisms*, 133–135.

6. *Isaiah 11:9; Habakkuk 2:14.*

TRUTH, BEAUTY, AND GOODNESS

Truth is *discovered* in the nature of reality (knowledge). Beauty is *uncovered* in the excellence latent in being (holiness). Goodness is *developed* in the excellence of being to ever-increasing degrees of perfection (righteousness). *Beauty* is the art of perfection; it is the mastery, and dominion of the nature of things as they attain their greatest expression in excellence (symmetry, unity, and completeness ordered as they should be). *Goodness* develops the powers latent in being in accordance with its nature, by performing its function.

The relationship between truth, beauty, and goodness is reflective of knowledge, holiness, and righteousness. It is grounded in our triune personality. The relationship is complex and dynamic. Knowledge leads to holiness: "Sanctify them [make them holy] by the truth; your word is truth" (Jn. 17:17). And knowledge and holiness lead to righteousness: "Then you will know the truth, and the truth will set you free" (Jn. 8:32). Holiness leads to knowledge: If we seek, we will understand, and "without holiness no one will see the Lord" (Heb. 12:14b). Righteousness leads to holiness: In trials, we become partakers of His holiness after we suffer, submit, and do what is right before God.

> Consider it pure joy, my brothers, whenever you face trials of many kinds, because you know that the testing of your faith develops perseverance. Perseverance must finish its work so that you may be mature and complete, not lacking anything (Jas. 1:2–4).

It is also true that righteousness leads to knowledge. "I consider that our present sufferings are not worth comparing with the glory that will be revealed in us" (Rom. 8:18).

HUMAN NATURE: AN ORDERED UNITY OF DIVERSITY

Man is made in the image of God, a unity of vast diversity discernible by the sevenfold layers of human nature. There are many kinds and levels of diversity in human nature, each capable of occasioning tensions within and between persons when what is more basic is not in place. There is real diversity among persons, but the diversity, when properly understood, is the basis for unity, not disunity.[7] There is a natural unity and a natural order for unity in each person, proceeding from intellect to emotion to will. Unity among persons begins with unity in a person. The seven aspects of human nature are ordered and, when understood contextually, attain brilliance shining forth manifesting *God's Grandeur*.[8]

1) Larger Aspect

Man is created finite, temporal, and changeable in his being, wisdom, power, holiness, justice, goodness, and truth. The larger aspect is universal and perpetual, in all persons at all times. The larger aspect is a formal aspect; its content is derived from man's heart, which is the narrower aspect. The formal aspect is not changeable by the Fall, redemption, or glorification.[9] Only the content of knowledge, holiness, and righteousness is changeable. The formal aspect requires content which must conform to the formal aspect.

---

7. Gangadean, *On Natural and Revealed Theology*, 33–39, 71–92, 107–118; Gangadean, "Paper No. 6: The Good," in *The Logos Papers*, 29–31.
8. Gerard Manley Hopkins. "God's Grandeur" Poetry Foundation. 2018. https://www.poetryfoundation.org/poems/44395/gods-grandeur.
9. Gangadean, *The Westminster Confession,* 138–142.

Man is the image of God and is distinct from the animals because he has qualities that God has and animals do not have. Man is the image of God and is distinct from God because he has natural attributes (being, wisdom, and power) and moral attributes (holiness, justice, goodness, and truth) in a finite, temporal, and changeable way. The attributes of God, which are infinite, eternal, and unchangeable, are incommunicable.[10] They cannot be shared with any creature, including man.

2) Narrower Aspect

Man is created a triune personality in the image of God.[11] Man is created in knowledge, holiness, and righteousness. These are distinct and inseparable. There is an order in their function. The narrower aspect gives content to the formal aspect. The heart is totally depraved[12] in extent; all aspects of man's heart are fallen and subject to ever-deeper depravity, but there are remnants of the original Edenic nature in the fallen man.

In our fallenness, man is changeable in the narrower aspect; he can change in knowledge, holiness, and righteousness. In knowledge, he can change from unbelief *to* belief and from misunderstanding *to* understanding and vice versa. In holiness, he can change from seeking his glory in devotion to the self *to* seeking the good in devotion to the knowledge of God. In righteousness, he can change from

---

10. Gangadean, *The Westminster Catechisms*, 119–122; Gangadean, *The Westminster Confession*, 47–52.

11. Gangadean, *The Westminster Confession*, 47–60.

12. Gangadean, *The Westminster Confession*, 99–110, 369–376; Gangadean, *The Westminster Catechisms*, 141–152.

obeying man-centered laws in autonomy *to* obeying God's law grounded in human nature.[13]

In regeneration, man is given a new heart. He is recreated in knowledge, holiness, and righteousness.[14] Remnants of the fallen nature continue after regeneration until death. No one is fully conscious and consistent in one's basic beliefs. There is an admixture of belief and unbelief, with one being more basic. The division in the regenerate arises from a war between the old unregenerate nature and the new regenerate nature. It is not a division between the aspects of man's heart nor between the heart and head.[15]

Division at the level of *presupposition* is in the area of epistemology (the basic things about God and man and good and evil are not clear to reason), metaphysics (it is not the case that only some is eternal), ethics (it is not the case that the good is the knowledge of God through the work of dominion).[16]

Division at the level of *mood* is vacillating between the old unregenerate nature and the new regenerate nature—at times, walking in the flesh and at times in the Spirit.[17] The old nature is centered on the autonomous self; the new nature is centered on God. The old nature loves the self more than God, and the new nature loves God more than

---

13. Gangadean, *Philosophical Foundation*, 171–284; Surrendra Gangadean, *History of Philosophy: A Critical Analysis of Unresolved Disputes* (Phoenix: Public Philosophy Press, 2022), 61–69; Gangadean, *The Westminster Catechisms*, 215–267; Gangadean, *The Westminster Confession,* 207–221; Gangadean, *On Natural and Revealed Theology*, 127–139, 166–178.

14. Gangadean, *The Westminster Confession,* 161–166.

15. Gangadean, *Philosophical Foundation*, 40–41; Gangadean, "Paper No. 120: Contra Voluntarism," in *The Logos Papers*, 611–647.

16. Gangadean, "Paper No. 1: The Logos Papers," 3–8; "Paper No. 15: Hermeneutics," 91–101; "Paper No. 76: Presupposition," in *The Logos Papers*, 397–399.

17. *Galatians 5:16–18.*

the self. Man is to love God with all his heart, mind, soul, and strength.[18] The new nature does not always prevail, but it ultimately does.[19]

3) Triune Personality

Man is created triune (intellect, emotion, and will) in the image of God. There is a natural order in the human personality between intellect, emotion, and will. In the economy of human personality, thought, feeling, and action are not independent. All living beings act; some beings that are sentient feel and act; only man thinks, feels, and acts. And in man, these three are ordered. What we think about the good directs desires and feelings. At least some feelings arise from belief systems, and others arise from intuition and from bodily states. Thought and feeling direct and move the will. Since thought directs the other aspects of feeling and will, the order can be spoken of as an order of authority. So, as far as the economy of the human personality is concerned, it can be said that the intellect rules.

One strand of diversity having an epistemological lifestyle implication is that of personality inclination. Some are inclined to the life of thought (reason), some to feeling (intuition), and some to action (sense experience). No one is exclusively one or the other, but one or the other is dominant in each person.

There is a recurrent recognition of the triune aspect of human personality in differing worldviews, which has been noted historically. In the ancient East, there was the yoga of knowledge (*jnana*), of love (*bhakti*), and of action (*karma*).

---

18. *Luke 10:27; Matthew 22:36–40; Mark 12:28–31.*
19. Gangadean, *The Westminster Confession,* 189–206; Gangadean, *The Westminster Catechisms,* 179–182.

The Hebrews recognized the functions of the prophet (brings the knowledge of God), priest (brings the people to holiness), and king (brings the people to righteousness). In the New Testament, there was conflict between those who follow Paul (prophetic), Apollos (priestly), or Cephas (kingly).[20] In the modern West, there was an age of Rationalism, Romanticism, and Pragmatism or Realism. In ethics, there is a distinction between is–want–ought, and between teleology (goal), consequentialism (happiness), and deontology (virtue). In the arts, between truth, beauty, and goodness. In psychology, Freud distinguished between the superego, id, and ego. In vocation, there are philosophers, artists, and businessmen. In regards to meaning, there is meaning as intelligibility, which precedes the need for meaning as significance, and meaning as purpose. Other sub-theories of personality are to be understood in light of the triune framework. Population divides among these lines: 90% are priestly/kingly and 10% prophetic. When distorted by sin, the diversity of functions (prophet, priest, and king) is a source of division in a group or culture.

4) Body/Soul Unity

The soul reveals God; the body reveals the soul, and there is an order between the two. Man is a unity of two distinct natures, the physical and the spiritual, in one person. Body and soul are a unity, and they affect each other. There is an order; the soul rules and leads the body in matters of knowledge, holiness, and righteousness.

---

20. *1 Corinthians 1:12–13.*

Body/soul unity is contrary to the following views:

1. Man is not a mere body with a mind reducible to the brain. Each is qualitatively different (thought vs. motion).[21]

2. Man is not a mere body without a soul as in naturalism. Man is a rational animal[22] crowned with glory and honor.[23]

3. Man is not a living being into which a soul is infused, as in theistic evolution. The soul has only one center of awareness; life and the soul are one and the same.[24]

4. Man is not a spirit temporarily imprisoned in a body, as in dualism. The body is not the source of evil.[25]

5. Man is not a soul transmigrating through innumerable bodies, as in reincarnation. If the soul was eternal, it would have infinite knowledge.[26]

6. Man is not an illusory self in an apparent body, as *atman* in Hinduism. Where does the illusion reside?[27]

7. Man is not a selfless being dependently co-arising, as *anatman* in Buddhism. Spirit is a substance with unity and continuity.[28]

---

21. Gangadean, *Philosophical Foundation*, 80–82.
22. Gangadean, "Paper No. 90: Christianity and Secular Humanism," in *The Logos Papers*, 473–477; Gangadean, *Philosophical Foundation*, 49–59.
23. *Psalm 8:5.*
24. Gangadean, *Philosophical Foundation*, 98–100.
25. Gangadean, *Philosophical Foundation*, 129–130.
26. Gangadean, *Philosophical Foundation*, 101–105, 130.
27. Gangadean, *Philosophical Foundation*, 111–112.
28. Gangadean, *Philosophical Foundation*, 66.

8. Man is not an eternal soul that eventually receives a body, as in Mormonism. There can be no unique event for eternal beings in time.[29]

9. Man is not a body shared with a nature-spirit as in animism. Man is a complete unity of body and soul; only man has conscious awareness.[30]

10. Man is not a trichotomy of body, spirit, and soul. The soul has thought, feeling, and will. The spirit is not other than the mind, which has understanding. [31]

Physical death is not original; it is imposed because of moral evil. Physical death is a reminder of spiritual death. Physical death is a call to stop and think; it is mercy, not justice. The physical and visible are used to signify the spiritual and the invisible. The soul does not cease to function when separated from the body. When moral evil is removed, then natural evil will be removed. The resurrection of the body completes redemption.

5) Male/Female Unity

Creation is revelation.[32] There is a creation order for understanding the relation between male and female. God is both male and female, masculine and feminine. Male and female are spiritual qualities since they are both in God. Man (male and female) is made in the image of God.[33] In God, the qualities of male and female are spiritual and distinct. God's

---

29. Gangadean, "Paper No. 76: Presupposition," in *The Logos Papers*, 397–399.
30. Gangadean, "Paper No. 125: Shamanism," in *The Logos Papers*, 659–660.
31. Gangadean, "Paper No. 122: Contra Charismatic Distinctive," in *The Logos Papers,* 653.
32. Gangadean, *The Biblical Worldview*, 21–36, 91–108.
33. *Genesis 1:26.*

masculine qualities are expressed in origination through creation. God's feminine qualities are expressed in providence through development by upholding, directing, disposing, governing, and ordering the creation. God's masculine and feminine qualities are equally in God; they are stunningly beautiful in their complementarity.

God is both Creator and upholder of all things. All humans—both men and women—are in the role of the feminine in relation to God. The invisible relation between God and man is revealed in the visible relation between man and woman. The work of initiating and originating is complemented and completed by the work of upholding and nurturing. The two distinct works are complementary and should not be separated. To have fruit, the work of planting and watering are both necessary and ordered, without the latter being subordinated to the former. In pursuit of the good, male and female exist in perfect unity. Without the good, there is no unity. Apart from the good, the antinomy of patriarchy and matriarchy arises and hinders the work of God.

Male and female are ordered. What was one (male and female principles in Adam) became two persons (Man and Woman), and what is two are to become one in marriage. Marriage is a full union of one man and one woman, which is monogamous and lasting.[34] Marriage is constituted by the full union of two persons, where the sexual union is the sign and seal of love. Marriage as a full union shares in purpose; marriage is for dominion, which is for the knowledge of God. Since each person is to seek to achieve the good, two persons in full union are all the more to seek to achieve the good. The increase of mankind is to the end of increasing the good. In families, we seek the good for and with children

---

34. Gangadean, *Philosophical Foundation*, 245–254.

and grandchildren, and succeeding generations, without end. Children are not the good but means to the good; companionship is not the good but the effect of mutually pursuing the good. Through marriage, succeeding generations expand in ever-enlarging communities, where material and spiritual riches accumulated over time are transmitted as inheritance. The continuation and completion of corporate, cumulative, and communal effort toward the good brings about the fullness of the good, which is comprehensive and inexhaustible.[35]

6) Background

Man is a temporal being. Man is born in a specific time and place amid many factors in history's outworking of the conflict between belief and unbelief. There are layers to our historical situatedness beginning with ancestry from either Shem, Ham, or Japheth;[36] ethnicity resulting from an admixture of races; epoch in redemptive history in which we are born (pre-Flood, post-Flood, under the Old Testament, at the time of Christ, in the apostolic age, early Church history, Middle Ages, the Reformation, the modern or postmodern world); station of development in a civilization in which we live whether early, middle, or late; cultural context of dominant ideology, whether the Age of Enlightenment, Romanticism, or Pragmatism/Realism; location within the *saeculum* or generational constellation,[37] whether idealist, reactive, civic, or adaptive; social movement, whether during a secular crisis or a spiritual awakening; belonging to a

---

35. Gangadean, *Philosophical Foundation*, 208–211.
36. Arthur C. Custance. *Noah's Three Sons: Human History in Three Dimensions* (Grand Rapids: Zondervan Pub. House, 1975).
37. William Strauss and Neil Howe. *Generations: The History of America's Future, 1584 to 2069* (New York: William Morrow, 1991).

cohort group subject to peer personality; phase of life in which we are and have undergone, whether youth, rising adult, midlife, or elderhood; birth order; upbringing, among many other factors.

7) Uniqueness

Man's uniqueness is irreducible to other aspects and factors of his being. Man's unique personality continues forever. It is expressed in the particularities of our being, analogous to the precious stones in the foundation of the City of God, which is seen as brilliance and magnificence expressed through our individuality; God is expressed in each individual human being in a unique way. Individual identities reach across centuries. Reason can grasp the abiding uniqueness of a particular—it can grasp the essence of Socrates, which characterizes Socrates through a lifetime of development and change, provided that the categories of analysis of personhood are sufficiently in place. The uniqueness of a person, for those who are attentive, can begin to manifest itself in the earliest infancy.

Differences among persons emerge from birth. They are not environmentally determined, but the extent of development is affected in part by one's total environment. As human beings develop, their uniqueness, interests, and abilities become more pronounced. Some aspects of reality capture one's interest. Interest leads to investigation and discovery and an ability to master relationships in the area of interest, which leads to greater interest, knowledge, and ability. Usually, this develops into one's area of specialization in education and career.

The uniqueness of our being is comprehensible in understanding all the particularities of our lives. Talent is grounded in the uniqueness of one's being and is in each person. The origin of talent, therefore, is from the origin of one's being. It is not from self, parents, or society. No one has, nor can have, all talent. One cannot achieve the fullness of the good by oneself, yet each one needs the good in its unity and fullness. Talent is given to each for the good, which is for all. Therefore, talent is given to each for all.

The uniqueness of one's personhood is developed upon the basis of which aspect of one's triune personality is dominant for that person: thought, feeling, or will. Talent, grounded in human personality, is to be classified according to the triune distinction in human personality.

Discernment is needed to classify talent appropriately. Faulty classification is both burdensome and oppressive. All philosophers are not the same. Within the field of philosophy, there are different areas, functions, and styles. Teaching philosophy is not doing philosophy. Scholastic system-building is not critiquing foundation. Intuitional approaches are not analytical approaches. Plato is not Aristotle; Kant is not Hegel; Descartes is not Derrida, in epistemological orientation. Yet all might agree on the need and desire to engage with basic questions using reason. An athlete who excels in action may do so because of "a fire in his belly." His talent is not to achieve excellence in act merely but to exhort others to excellence, knowing that fire motivates from deep within.

Talent does not originate by human will but is developed by human will. More often than not, talent is hardly developed due to lack of human will. Parents and teachers, given the limits of circumstances and worldview, discern and develop talent in its early stages. Personal desire and effort complete its development. The accumulated cultural achievement, both material and intellectual, is the base from which one begins development. Poverty, in both senses, hinders development of talent. All families and cultures are not equally endowed, and some worldviews are inimical to development. For what a person achieves, there is a debt owed to one's forebears, and through them, to all mankind. But personal effort is essential in order to go further than current levels of cultural achievement, and to add to it. And society in turn owes a debt to that person.

In a society well endowed with opportunities for development through education, a person may neglect those opportunities or not use them fully to develop one's talent. Persons with the highest education in the highest offices may fail to come to a knowledge of the good. Therefore, talent, which is an ability to achieve some aspect of the good, fails to be exercised toward the good, and so comes short of its fullest development and achievement. Pressing challenges to achieving the good are ignored or avoided because the goal of the good is not in view. Without belief that basic things are clear, reason will not be exercised to show this clarity. Without insight, confidence, and compassion, a researcher will not persevere to achieve a medical breakthrough. Faith as understanding and insight, hope as confidence that the problems can be solved, and love as compassion for those who suffer, are virtues necessary to achieve the good and to find the means to it.

Talent is irrepressible. When it is fully developed, it forms its function. It finds ways to come to expression in service to others. Talent not only survives; it cuts new channels; it devises new ways to express itself, and it overcomes. Uniqueness expressed through maturity reaches perfection, power, and strength. The development of talent is the expression of dominion, the achievement of mastery. It is accomplished not in an abstract, theoretical manner but in the context of love, that is, in seeking the good for others.

Appendix B

Philosophy of Art Outline

1. Art is revelation of being by humans (word/logos vs. natural, mere copy, or merely expressive, or moving/pleasing).

2. Art is about humans, for all humans, about the universal human condition (sin and death, toil, division, strife, war, self-love, pride, etc.).

3. Art is expressed through a concrete particular: objective correlative (art uses natural signs/symbols to communicate). The visible reveals the invisible: creation/Creator, body/soul, soul/God.

4. Art is grasped by intuitive awareness: direct/immediate perception of natural signs that express the universal (vs. conventional).

5. Art is received–perceived–conceived (from the more basic to the less basic).

6. Art is interpreted through hard work in much discussion, addressing challenges to get to assumptions. Art is clear at the basic level, like the existence and nature of God.

7. Artistic works have unity (aseity) and self-sufficiency (pure and entire). They show, don't tell—not mean but be. Artistic works have perspicuity/transparency in the public eye vs. gnosticism in either historical, biographical, or technical knowledge.

8. Art is done in the context of dominion in the humanities. Truth-beauty-goodness, knowledge-holiness-righteousness (in that order).

9. Art is done in the context of the beauty of holiness: the yearning for the ideal, perfection, and completeness.

10. All beautiful things are perfect. All perfect things are beautiful. All perfection (making perfect) is achieved by art through mastery and dominion. Because art is aimed at perfection, beauty is the art of perfection.

11. Feeling is a function of worldview (presupposition and system), personality, background, and mood.

12. Objectivity is grounded in the above standards, held more or less consciously and consistently. It is known by those who know the human condition (moral rule), those who attain maturity in the biblical worldview of creation–fall–redemption, and those who know the symbols (maturity and natural rule).

Selected Bibliography

Allen, Don C. *The Harmonious Vision: Studies in Milton's Poetry.* Baltimore, 1954.

Bodkin, Maud. *Archetypal Patterns in Poetry: Psychological Studies of Imagination.* Oxford University Press, 1934.

Bowra, C. M. *From Virgil to Milton.* London, 1945.

Bradshaw, John. *Concordance to Milton.* Hamden, Conn., 1965.

Broadbent, J. B. *Some Graver Subject: An Essay on Paradise Lost.* London, 1960.

Burden, Dennis H. *The Logical Epic.* Cambridge, 1967.

Bush, Douglas. *Paradise Lost in Our Time. Some Comments.* London: Milford, 1945.

Bush, Douglas. *John Milton: A Sketch of his Life and Writings.* New York, 1964.

Bush, Douglas. *English Literature In The Earlier Seventeenth Century.* Oxford, 1945.

Cope, Jackson I. *The Metaphoric Structure of Paradise Lost.* Baltimore, 1962.

Diekhoff, John S. *Milton's Paradise Lost, A Commentary on the Argument.* New York, 1946.

Eliot, T. S. *On Poetry and Poets.* London, 1957.

Empson, William. *Milton's God.* London, 1962.

Ferry, Anne Davidson. *Milton's Epic Voice: The Narrator in Paradise Lost.* Cambridge, Mass., 1963.

Fish, Stanley E. *Surprised by Sin.* New York, 1967.

Gardner, Helen. *A Reading of Paradise Lost.* Oxford, 1965.

Hamilton, G. Rostrevor. *Hero or Fool? A Study of Milton's Satan.* London, 1944.

Hanford, James Holly. "The Temptation Motive in Milton." *Studies in Philology,* XV (1918), 176-194.

Hughes, Merritt Y. *Ten Perspectives on Milton.* London, 1965.

Kermode, Frank L. "Adam Unparadised." *The Living Milton: Essays by Various Hands.* London, 1960.

Kranidas, Thomas. *The Fierce Equation.* The Hague, 1965.

Leavis, F. R. *The Common Pursuit.* London, 1952.

Lewis, C. S. *A Preface to Paradise Lost.* London, 1942.

Lovejoy, Arthur O. "Milton and the Paradox of the Fortunate Fall." *Essays in the History of Ideas.* Baltimore, 1948.

MacCaffrey, Isabel Gamble. *Paradise Lost as Myth.* Cambridge, Mass., 1959.

Marilla, Esmond L. *The Central Problem of Paradise Lost: The Fall of Man.* Cambridge, Mass., 1953.

Milton, John. *Complete Poems and Major Prose.* ed. Merritt Y. Hughes. New York, 1957.

Murray, P. *Milton: The Modern Phase.* New York, 1967.

Nicolson, Marjorie Hope. *John Milton: A Reader's Guide to His Poetry.* New York, 1963.

Patrides, C. A. *Milton and the Christian Tradition.* New York, 1966.

Peter, John. *A Critique of Paradise Lost.* New York, 1960.

Prince, F. T. "On the Last Two Books of Paradise Lost." *Essays and Studies,* XI, (1958), 38-52.

Rajan, B. *Paradise Lost and the Seventeenth Century Reader.* London, 1962.

Raleigh, Sir Walter S. *Milton.* London, 1900.

Ricks, Christopher. *Milton's Grand Style.* Oxford, 1963.

Schultz, Howard. *Milton and Forbidden Knowledge.* New York, 1955.

Steadman, John M. "Archangel to Devil: The Background of Satan's Metamorphosis." *Modern Language Quarterly,* XXI (1960), 321-335.

Stein, Arnold. *Answerable Style: Essays on Paradise Lost.* Minneapolis, 1953.

Stoll, Elmer E. "Give the Devil His Due: A Reply to Mr. Lewis." *Review of English Studies,* XX (1944), 108-124.

Summers, Joseph H. *The Muse's Method: An Introduction to Paradise Lost.* Cambridge, Mass., 1962.

Tillyard, E. M. W. *Milton.* Revised ed. New York, 1967.

Waldock, A. J. *Paradise Lost and Its Critics.* Cambridge, 1947.

Werblowsky, R. J. Zwi. *Lucifer and Prometheus: A Study of Milton's Satan.* London, 1952.

Whaler, James. "The Miltonic Simile." *PMLA,* XLVI (1931), 1034-1074.

Williams, Charles. "Milton." *The English Poetic Mind.* Oxford, (1932), 110-152.

Wright, B. A. *Milton's Paradise Lost: A Reassessment of the Poem.* New York, 1962.

About the Author

DR. SURRENDRA GANGADEAN (1943–2022) was a Professor of Philosophy at Phoenix College and at Paradise Valley Community College for 45 years. Additionally, he taught from the pulpit at Westminster Fellowship for almost 30 years and taught courses at Logos Theological Seminary for over 25 years. Courses he taught include: Introduction to Philosophy, Logic, Ethics, Philosophy of Religion, Eastern Religions, World Religions, Introduction to Christianity, Introduction to Humanities, Philosophy of Art, The Great Books, Philosophical Theology, Biblical Worldview, Biblical History, Church History, Systematic Theology, Biblical Hermeneutics, and Existential Hermeneutics. He received an M.A. degree in Literature from the Arizona State University, an M.A. degree in Philosophy from the University of Arizona, and a Ph.D. in Natural Theology from Reformed International Theological Seminary. He presented academic papers and public lectures on Natural Theology and the Moral Law. Dr. Gangadean was the organizing Pastor of Westminster Fellowship church, and President of The Logos Foundation, which serves academic education in Liberal Arts and Theology.